MUSIC

THE FAITHFUL LEARNING SERIES

An Invitation to Academic Studies, Jay D. Green
Chemistry, Daniel R. Zuidema
Literature, Clifford W. Foreman
Music, Timothy H. Steele
Philosophy, James S. Spiegel
Political Science, Cale Horne
Sociology, Matthew S. Vos

JAY D. GREEN, SERIES EDITOR

MUSIC

Timothy H. Steele

P U B L I S H I N G
P.O. BOX 817 • PHILLIPSBURG • NEW JERSEY 08865-0817

Library of Congress Cataloging-in-Publication Data

Names: Steele, Timothy Howard, author.
Title: Music / Timothy H. Steele.
Description: Phillipsburg : P&R Publishing, 2016. | Series: The faithful learning series | Includes bibliographical references.
Identifiers: LCCN 2016001638| ISBN 9781596389120 (pbk.) | ISBN 9781596389137 (epub) | ISBN 9781596389144 (mobi)
Subjects: LCSH: Music--Religious aspects--Christianity.
Classification: LCC ML3921.2 .S74 2016 | DDC 780.2/423--dc23
LC record available at http://lccn.loc.gov/2016001638

Music is a science that wants us to laugh, and sing, and dance.

—GUILLAUME DE MACHAUT[1]

MUSIC IS A SCIENCE—a scholarly discipline worthy of study and reflection. And it is also an art that entertains us, helps us to worship, cheers us up when we're feeling low, and nourishes our hearts and minds over a lifetime. We study music because, as human beings, we are made to be music makers and music listeners, dancers and singers and players of instruments. I often point out to my students that the first recorded words of Adam are a song celebrating his union with Eve: "This is now bone of my bones and flesh of my flesh" (Gen. 2:23); and that the prophet Zephaniah pictured even God himself as a singer who rejoices over his bride: "The LORD your God is with you, he is mighty to save. He will take great delight in you, he will quiet you with his love, he will rejoice over you with singing" (Zeph. 3:17).

Christians over the centuries have used music to help them pray, to celebrate weddings, and to add solemnity to funerals. And they have had much to say about music—what it is, what it is useful for, and how we ought to think about it. For many, music is something to celebrate. Martin Luther called it "a fine, delightful gift, that has often roused and moved me, and won me over to the joy of preaching."[2] But

---

1. Guillaume de Machaut (ca. 1300–1377) was the foremost musician and poet of fourteenth-century France. A modern edition of his "Prologue" is available in Oeuvres de Guillaume de Machaut, ed. Ernest Hoepffner (Paris: Librairie de Firmin-Didot, 1908), 1:9, available online at http://www.archive.org/stream /uvresdeguillaum00guilgoog#page/n111/mode/2up. The English translation is my own.

2. Martin Luther, *D. Martin Luthers Werke: Tischreden*, vol. 4, 1538–1540

Christians have also insisted that music was caught up in the fall along with everything else. Both Luther and John Calvin were concerned about the potential that music has to become a corrupting influence, and in his preface to the first book of Genevan psalms Calvin warned against an overly optimistic view of music: "As wine is poured into the cask with a funnel, so venom and corruption are distilled to the very depths of the heart by melody."[3]

Music is a powerful medium. It helps people to get a feeling across or add significance to what they want to say. But sometimes what people say with music is full of violence and hate, which is a problem because music underscores the potency of words with special vividness through its patterning of sound and time. In Genesis we read how Lamech boasted of murder and flaunted God's redemptive promises. But although the text refers to him *saying* these horrible things to his wives, the lyrical structure indicates that his words were preserved as a song.

> Lamech said to his wives,
> "Adah and Zillah, listen to me;
>> wives of Lamech, hear my words.
> I have killed a man for wounding me,
>> a young man for injuring me.
> If Cain is avenged seven times,
>> then Lamech seventy-seven times." (Gen. 4:23–24)

In fact, music seems to attach itself to anything that the sinful human heart is able to come up with.

(Weimar: Hermann Böhlau Nachfolger, 1916), 314, http://www.archive.org/stream /werketischreden10204luthuoft#page/314/mode/2up.

3. John Calvin, "Epistle to the Reader," *The Geneva Psalter* (1543), trans. Oliver Strunk, in Oliver Strunk, ed., *Source Readings in Music History*, rev. ed., Leo Treitler, general ed. (New York: W. W. Norton, 1998), 366.

Despite this, generalizations that associate certain musical sounds with human sinfulness can be misleading and must be thought through carefully. We ought to avoid confusing pleasantness with beauty or thinking that dissonance in music is itself sinful even though discord in human relations may well be. Nevertheless, the true consequences of the fall show up when we consider how apparently normal people have *used* music, even music that most would say is beautiful, to accompany mass murder or to inflict injury.[4] In all this, Christians stubbornly maintain that the materials of music, and the human abilities associated with music making, are gifts of God—parts of his *good* creation. We insist that people should be responsible, that they ought to make good and wise use of these gifts. Along with this, we want musicians to sing about justice and peace and the gospel message of grace, and we want musicians to use music to serve their neighbors, especially the poor and the oppressed, as stewards of sound in the kingdom of God.[5] We need performers, composers, and musicologists who understand all facets of music in human life and who apply their minds and their talents to the task of renewing this complex musical world.

This booklet is intended to help those who want to study music and use their gifts for the glory of God, especially those who are or may become music majors in college. At its core are two important questions that students ought to ask: In view of all the challenges involved, will my study of music help me to love and serve God better?

---

4. Benita Wolters-Fredlund, "Experiencing Beauty in the Music of the Holocaust," *The Cresset* 72, no. 4 (Easter 2009): 21–31, http://thecresset.org/2009/Easter /wolters-fredlund.html. See also Bruce Johnson and Martin Cloonan, *Dark Side of the Tune: Popular Music and Violence* (Farnham, UK: Ashgate, 2009), 150–60.

5. Karen A. DeMol, *Sound Stewardship: How Shall Christians Think About Music?* (Sioux Center, IA: Dordt College Press, 1999), 22–23.

Can my learning in the discipline of music help me to live more faithfully? I believe the answer to both questions is a resounding yes! But before we jump in, it's important to take some soundings and see how deep and wide this marvelous academic discipline is—this "science," as Machaut called it. I want to show you what musicians think about and why such things matter. We'll take a look at some pretty big issues (musical meaning, for instance) as well as listen in on a very old conversation about how music reflects and embodies the order of creation. And along the way I'll highlight perspectives that may help us to think about how the study of music is part of God's provision for our spiritual formation.

WHAT IS THE DISCIPLINE OF MUSIC?

In Praise of the Almighty's will, and for my neighbor's greater skill.

—J. S. BACH[6]

In my years of teaching in Christian colleges I've found that students are often confused about musical study. They love music and want it to be part of their lives, but they may not understand how music works as an academic discipline. Many are outstanding performers but have never studied music theory, while others are experienced worship leaders who have had no formal training in music at all. Faced with several years' worth of courses that seem to have little to do with the music they love, some withdraw from the major or choose not to begin it at all. I recall struggling

---

6. From the title page of the *Little Organ Book* (Orgelbüchlein), BWV 599–644. Translated by Arthur Mendel in Hans T. David and Arthur Mendel, eds., *The Bach Reader: A Life of Johann Sebastian Bach in Letters and Documents*, rev. ed. (New York: W. W. Norton, 1966), 75.

as a college music major to understand the academic side of music, especially the required music theory and music history courses. It was difficult for me to accept explanations as to why these were necessary or what I might gain from the time and effort invested in them. Of course, not every student struggles with these things, then or now. But as I write these sentences I'm reminded just how often I meet students in my classes who have never really thought about what the discipline of music is or what the real value of musical study in college might be.

Ethnomusicologist Bonnie C. Wade challenges us to begin by thinking about who musicians are and what they do.

> Music makers are individuals and groups, adults and children, female and male, amateurs and professionals. They are people who make music only for themselves, such as shower singers or secretly-sing-along-with-the-radio types, and they are performers, people who make music purposefully for others. They are people who make music because they are required to and people who do so simply from desire. Some music makers study seriously, while others are content to make music however they can, without special effort.[7]

Viewed from this angle, all people are musicians, because all people make music meaningful and useful in their lives.[8] But some choose to apply themselves to the study of music in a way that goes beyond the everyday. People who make music "purposefully" and study music "seriously" may be said to engage in the *discipline* of music. In her short

---

7. Bonnie C. Wade, *Thinking Musically: Experiencing Music, Expressing Culture,* 3rd ed. (New York: Oxford University Press, 2012), 1.
8. Ibid., 1–6.

story about a neighbor who tries to teach a stone to talk, Annie Dillard offers a useful picture of this kind of work. "I assume," she writes, "that like any other meaningful effort, the ritual involves sacrifice, the suppression of self-consciousness, and *a certain precise tilt of the will*, so that the will becomes transparent and hollow, a channel for the work."[9] Over time this "precise tilt of the will" becomes second nature, and the tasks of coming up with new and well-made music—working through the problems of understanding how a complex piece of music means what we think it does; performing a masterpiece from the past with commitment and intelligence—begin to shape a musician's mind and heart according to the contours of the discipline. Musicians who devote themselves to this kind of study become practitioners of the discipline of music, and the content of that discipline, as well as all the practices associated with it, become their responsibility.

Three Musical Practices

As those who pursue this calling out of love for Jesus Christ, then, we ought to think about what the lineaments of the discipline are so that we can better understand how students and scholars alike are being formed by this learning. One simple way to do this is to divide the discipline into three broad fields or practices: performance, composition, and musicology. We'll take a look at each in turn.

Performance is the musical practice that most people are familiar with. It is what we mostly think of when we form a picture of music making in our minds. All music students know that learning to perform well means many years of private lessons and countless hours of lonely practice. But

9. Annie Dillard, "Teaching a Stone to Talk," in *Teaching a Stone to Talk: Expeditions and Encounters* (New York: Harper Perennial, 1992), 86 (emphasis added).

the best performers also learn that they need to be open not only to their own individual achievement but also to values shaped in community, through participation in ensembles of diverse kinds. Performers give music a public face—they are the musicians who many students aspire to become.

Music composition is also both an individual and a corporate activity. Composers often work on commission or as part of a team (as with film scoring or creating music for video games). They are songwriters and jazz improvisers, and they compose operas and commercial jingles. Success in the craft of composition requires a love for new music of all kinds, as well as a solid foundation in a particular musical language, whether classical or popular. Often composers are consulted for their views on music, and many of the most important insights into the nature and structure of music have come from them.

The third practice, musicology, requires somewhat more explanation. I use the term *musicology* to refer to the scholarly study of music in general, encompassing music theory, analysis, the writing of music history, and ethnomusicology, together with various hybrids and interdisciplinary subdivisions that comprise the broad field of academic studies in music. As the musical practice most closely aligned with the liberal arts in the modern university, musicology provides the clearest linkage between the study of music and the other disciplines. Most of the discussion that follows will have musicology in view. But I want to affirm before we get into the details that the discipline of music, being in truth a multidisciplinary field, cannot be comprehended by any one of the three practices alone. Deep within the DNA of the discipline of music is the idea that the true musician possesses a well-rounded knowledge of and experience in all three practices, even as she may find her place in God's world as a practitioner of mainly one.

What gives the discipline its coherence in an academic context is that performers, composers, and musicologists have each, in their diverse ways, contended with the same issues and asked many of the same questions. Musicians have thought long and hard about the fact that music has much in common with mathematics, for instance—that it both reflects and embodies a kind of order. And, as we learn from scholars like Bonnie Wade, *people* make music meaningful as well as useful.[10] That is, music is significant, and the way that people use it affects what they understand it to mean. So in order to provide a framework for our discussion, I will focus on three musical themes that I believe have had not only a profound influence on the discipline of music in the past, but also a continuing ability to provoke conversations about music today.

Three Musical Themes

The capstone course for music majors at Calvin College, which I teach, is called simply, "Order, Meaning, and Function." It serves as both the senior seminar for the music department and an integrative studies course in the core curriculum. As a course designed to help students to integrate their Christian faith with their learning in the discipline of music, it offers a chance for students to find connections among all the things they've read and thought about and experienced during their time in college. Together we challenge one another to envision our learning in terms of God's call to faithful service and stewardship in his kingdom.

Order, meaning, and function are concepts that help us to think about and think through this challenge to live faithfully in God's world as musicians. When we talk about these themes and the many musical conversations that cluster

10. Wade, *Thinking Musically*, 10–19.

around them, we treat them not as mere abstractions or foundations for research projects, but as biblically grounded insights that compel us to make choices about music and about our lives. A brief look at each theme in its biblical context will help us to be similarly grounded as we try to engage more deeply with the questions of the discipline.

The first of the three themes, *order*, invites us to connect music with the doctrine of creation. The Bible reveals God as the one who *makes* the world and populates it with creatures, who *cares* about the world, and who *sustains* the world through Jesus Christ. Psalm 8 pictures an ordered creation: "When I consider your heavens, the work of your fingers, the moon and the stars, which you have set in place" (Ps. 8:3); and Hebrews 1 points to the Christological significance of creation, linking the order of heaven to the dynamic movement of time toward its end:

> The Son is the radiance of God's glory and the exact representation of his being, sustaining all things by his powerful word. After he had provided purification for sins, he sat down at the right hand of the Majesty in heaven. So he became as much superior to the angels as the name he has inherited is superior to theirs. (Heb. 1:3–4)

For thousands of years musicians have noticed that music both reflects and embodies these aspects of creation—that it is ordered, in the sense of exhibiting a harmonious design, and that it embodies an ordered process that unfolds in time. The connection of these things to musical uses of sound and time brings us into the general conversation about music theory.

The second theme, *meaning*, has to do with the interpretation of music—our ways of construing what it means to us. It is easy to understand how the arts in general, and music in particular, may be said to make life more meaningful, endowing certain occasions with a significance they might not otherwise have. And the Bible reminds us that "the heavens *declare* the glory of God" and that the creation was made by God to have a voice, to "pour forth *speech*" day by day (Ps. 19:1–2). Christians refer to this testimony as general revelation, and human music making has a place in that chorus of praise.[11] The real challenge for musicians is to understand how musical meaning happens and to reflect on what music is capable of saying.

The third and final theme is *function*. Scripture is rich in descriptions of music as a social practice: Miriam playing the tambourine as she leads the Israelite women in a celebration dance (Ex. 15:20), or David playing his harp as King Saul "was prophesying in his house" (1 Sam. 18:10). And rather than thinking about historical or cultural context merely as a background against which "music" is set as an object of contemplation, many musicologists today are trying to understand the cultural and social work that music does. This way of thinking has enriched the discipline by bringing a lot of music and music making into the conversation that was marginalized—or even ignored—by scholars of earlier generations.

Before we go on I want to stress that my purpose in arranging the discussion around these themes is not so much to explore the themes themselves but to enable us to focus on the questions that musicians and scholars ask; for it is these questions, as I've said, that give coherence to the discipline. This is not a formal treatise on musical scholarship; rather it's an introduction to the busy world of disciplined thinking about music and disciplined music

---

11. Jeremy S. Begbie, *Resounding Truth: Christian Wisdom in the World of Music* (Grand Rapids: Baker Academic, 2007), 202.

making. What I hope is that a sense of the vitality and richness of the discipline will emerge as we look more deeply into these questions.

ORDER

> The heavens declare the glory of God; the skies proclaim the work of his hands. (Ps. 19:1)

One of the best known choruses from Joseph Haydn's oratorio *The Creation* (1797) sets the opening words of Psalm 19 in a style that musicologists refer to as "the classical style," employing a distinctive approach to rhythm, melody, and harmony that foregrounds such characteristic ordering features as formal symmetry, balanced phrases, regular accents, and a unified tonality (in this case, C major). In the hands of a master craftsman in this style, as Haydn certainly was, music such as this appeals to us on a deeper level than merely as a vehicle for the psalm text. Even as we hear the words of the chorus express the psalmist's awe and wonder at the fact that God's glory is revealed through the majestic order of creation, we are aware that the music Haydn wrote to set those words also testifies to the glory of God through its *musically* ordered structures of sound and time.

This ability of music to sound out the order of creation need not be seen as limited to any particular style; and neither, I would maintain, is it unique to one period of music history or one human culture. Musicians everywhere are engaged with the given material of creation—the facts of sound and time and the meaningful patterns that reflect human life. Jeremy Begbie refers to these things, significantly, as a "sonic order" comprised of what he calls "integrities of . . . sound-producing materials, sound waves, human bodies, and time" together with "the patterns of sounds that make up music."[12] What musicians must come to understand is that there is a reciprocity between human creative activity and the creation: we are part of the creation, but as his image bearers we have been given the task by God of respecting, developing, and stewarding it for his glory and for our good use.[13] This is why musicians work hard to get their music to come out right, to make "sense" in some way. In addition to trusting their own intuitions, then, musicians must engage in some music theory: investigating the properties of sound that are musically useful, for instance, or analyzing the way in which rhythm and meter shape our expectations. The roots of this disciplined thinking extend to the most ancient records of human culture.

The earliest surviving instructions for tuning a lyre, discovered on a clay tablet from Ugarit dated to approximately 1400–1250 BC, offer insight into the way that musicians think systematically about the musical concept of pitch.[14] Much as any musician needs to know some basic music theory in order to confront the present-day challenge of tuning a guitar or violin, this early practical theory of music showed how to obtain usable musical pitches by selecting, from among an infinite number of potential sounds, just those that go together well (musicians refer to this as *consonance*). The resulting series or order is a kind of tonal system, which can be represented by a scale (all the pitches assembled in order from low to high).

Greek music theorists of the fifth and fourth centuries BC also wrote about the practical problems of tuning. And

12. Ibid., 49.
13. Ibid., 207–8.
14. Anne D. Kilmer, Richard L. Crocker, and Robert R. Brown, *Sounds from Silence: Recent Discoveries in Ancient Near East Music*, recorded lecture demonstration, BTNK 101, 1976, 33 1/3 rpm LP, 2 compact discs.

they had much to say about rhythm and meter, the characteristics of a good composition, and how music affects human character as well as individual and group behavior. But among the most enduring of ancient Greek musical ideas is the association of music with number, derived from the teachings of Pythagoras (late sixth century BC). Pythagoras reasoned that the entire cosmos may be understood by means of numbers, and tradition assigned to him the discovery that musical pitches could be generated by dividing a string according to simple mathematical ratios. This correspondence between music and the universe gave impetus to one of the most powerful metaphors in human history: the harmony of the spheres.[15] Since the motions and distances of the heavenly bodies were thought to be governed by mathematical proportions—just like the pitches and rhythms of music—both were understood to exhibit the fundamental unity and coherence of harmony.

The heritage of Greek musical speculation and inquiry was passed to the musicians of the Middle Ages, and, over time, Greek ideas about the mathematical basis of harmony, along with many other insights into the nature of music from the ancient world, became the intellectual property of Europe. Music was taught in cathedral schools and universities as part of the quadrivium of subjects (along with arithmetic, geometry, and astronomy) that make up the mathematical side of the seven liberal arts.[16] Music thus became part of the rational foundations of learning in the Western tradition.

The Enlightenment stimulated interest in the empirical theory of music, which is rooted in sense experience. As

15. J. Peter Burkholder, Donald Jay Grout, and Claude V. Palisca, *A History of Western Music*, 8th ed. (New York: W. W. Norton, 2010), 13.

16. Theodore C. Karp, "Music," in *The Seven Liberal Arts in the Middle Ages*, ed. David L. Wagner (Bloomington, IN: Indiana University Press, 1986), 169–95.

the music of Haydn, Mozart, Beethoven, and their contemporaries became established as a classical style in the late eighteenth and early nineteenth centuries, the concept of *tonality* provided a means to account for the way certain aspects of music are heard. Music was regarded as tonal if it was composed in one of the twenty-four major and minor keys.[17] In an early nineteenth-century textbook on musical composition, one finds this description of the most characteristic property of tonality, at the head of a chapter on "keys":

> When our ear perceives a succession of tones and harmonies, it naturally endeavors to find amidst this multiplicity and variety an internal connection—a relationship to a common central point. . . . The ear . . . longs to perceive some tone as a principal and central tone, some harmony as a principal harmony, around which the others revolve as accessories around their principal, to wit, around the predominant harmony.[18]

Gottfried Weber's reliance on what the ear perceives, and his way of accounting for the pull of music towards a center, which he called "tonic," enabled theoretical accounts of harmony to connect with the way that we listen to symphonies and other large-scale works. This way of thinking continues to inform the teaching of music theory in present-day college classrooms. For example, a widely used textbook introduces the concept of tonal harmony with reference to a

---

17. On tonality as part of a musical "language," see Charles Rosen, *The Classical Style: Haydn, Mozart, Beethoven,* expanded ed. (New York: W. W. Norton, 1998), 19–29.

18. Gottfried Weber, *Theory of Musical Composition: Treated with a View to a Naturally Consecutive Arrangement of Topics,* trans. James F. Warner (Boston: Oliver Ditson, 1846), 1:254–55.

"tonal center" that provides "a sense of gravity."[19] It should not escape our notice that this property of having a center around which everything revolves, or toward which things pull, is a highly suggestive metaphor for the creation itself.

Tonality is the basis for an influential theory of musical analysis called *Schenkerian analysis*, derived from the work of the Austrian music theorist Heinrich Schenker. Schenkerian analysis assumes that music embodies a composite melodic/harmonic structure in which a stepwise descending fundamental line is combined with a bass arpeggiation. Together these two elements constitute the fundamental structure of the work.[20] This is clearly an extension of the idea of tonality itself as the perceptible pull of music toward a central tone. But Schenker's theory of tonality introduces a new concept, which can best be understood through its most characteristic feature: the graphic representation of various levels of a work's tonal structure. Here the surface of the music is connected to a theorized background level that exerts a kind of structural authority over the music's audible form. The theory explains how to discover and graphically represent these structural relationships, and a detailed analysis thus becomes a compelling explanation of how a piece of music may be experienced as manifesting both a simple and logical order and a dynamic, goal-directed process.[21] Many of Schenker's own analyses are beautiful objects of design in their own right, and it is worth noting that one unique trait of such analyses is that they do not need much verbal description to be understood if the

19. Stefan Kostka and Dorothy Payne, *Tonal Harmony: With an Introduction to Twentieth-Century Music*, 6th ed. (Boston: McGraw-Hill Higher Education, 2009), xi.

20. Allen Forte and Steven E. Gilbert, *Introduction to Schenkerian Analysis* (New York: W. W. Norton, 1982), 132.

21. Nicholas Cook, *A Guide to Musical Analysis* (London: J. M. Dent & Sons, 1987; repr., New York: W. W. Norton, 1992), 57–66.

reader is well trained in the symbols being used. In this way Schenker essentially created a new way of notating musical experience, not as a record of how to perform a piece of music, but as a model for hearing it.[22]

One of the challenges that faced twentieth-century theorists was how to think about and explain *atonal* music— music that deliberately avoids any sense of tonality. The first examples of this new style of music were composed by Arnold Schoenberg toward the end of the first decade of the twentieth century. In atonal music, dissonance is treated with maximum freedom, negating the pull toward the tonic that characterizes tonality. What is now called *set theory*, developed by American music theorists in the second half of the century, provides a model to explain how groups of pitches (called *pitch-class sets*) may be shown to be related— and thus, we might add, how they exhibit traces of the old notion of harmony—even though they occur in a piece that studiously avoids the melodic and harmonic conventions of tonality.[23] Since atonal music lacks the gravitational pull toward the tonic that shapes tonal music, set theory is really a different kind of theory than Schenkerian analysis and rests on a rational and intellectual—rather than an empirical and experiential—foundation. Whereas a good Schenkerian analysis ought to help us to hear a piece of music better (or at least in a new way), analyses produced according to set theory yield abstract relationships that need not be audible in the music as performed.[24] What is thus genuinely intriguing about set theory is that it again organizes musical thought under a form of mathematics,

22. Ibid., 67.

23. A practical introduction to set theory is Joseph N. Straus, *Introduction to Post-Tonal Theory*, 2nd ed. (Upper Saddle River, NJ: Prentice Hall, 2000), 1–111.

24. Cook, *Guide to Musical Analysis*, 120–21. Cook calls this kind of analysis "formal" as opposed to "psychological."

adopting an even stricter rationalism than had dominated Western musical theory since Pythagoras.

MEANING

What the music I love expresses to me are thoughts not too indefinite for words, but rather too definite.
—FELIX MENDELSSOHN[25]

The conceptual differences between Schenkerian analysis and set theory raise a number of questions that shift our discussion from order to meaning in music. Is music best understood as a medium for expressing ideas through metaphor (thus becoming "goal driven"), or can it refer to things more directly? Are the feelings we have when we listen to music based on something in the music itself? Or is music just abstract relationships among tones ordered in a purely formal way? Is a musical work a text to be interpreted? Or is it a way of reasoning tied to mathematics and symbolic logic?

As I mentioned before, Christians generally affirm that human music making is part of the creation's testimony to God's glory and that it embodies the order of creation in unique ways. But when asked what a specific symphony means, or what a long bluesy solo by Eric Clapton says, can we give an answer that will persuade anyone but ourselves? The existence of a composer's program may suggest limits to the range of possible meanings in purely instrumental music, but in many cases one can simply throw the program away and still have a meaningful experience of the work. It would seem obvious that texted music would present fewer

25. Felix Mendelssohn, letter to Marc-André Souchay, October 15, 1842, trans. John Michael Cooper, in Strunk, *Source Readings in Music History*, 1201. Italics in original.

problems of interpretation, but works such as Beethoven's song cycle *An die ferne Geliebte* and "Close to the Edge" by the progressive rock band Yes suggest otherwise to me. So when we disagree about what music means, how do we decide whose interpretation is most likely to be right? Is there any objective reality to musical meaning, or is it all merely subjective?

Musicians who struggle with these things are in good company. For some, theories of musical meaning that link musical structures directly to extra-musical ideas or emotional states are inherently controversial. But such theories have nonetheless arisen at key points in Western musical history. The theory of affects (emotional states) and the *Figurenlehre* (a system of musical symbols) supplied musicians with practical techniques for using music to point to or embody specific meanings. In the music of Bach and other German composers of the early eighteenth century, one can see and hear how certain musical constructions (melodic motives, for instance) constitute a kind of rhetoric, as described in theoretical works such as Johann Mattheson's *Der vollkommene Capellmeister* ("The Complete Chapel Master," 1739), and consequently such figures should in principle be taken into account in any interpretation of the music.[26] Yet, even though such ideas are useful for thinking about early eighteenth-century music, few musicologists would accept them today as a general theory of musical meaning.

A notable advocate of the skeptical side was Eduard Hanslick, an influential nineteenth-century Viennese music critic who was an outspoken opponent of what he considered extravagant claims about musical meaning. For Hanslick, beauty and meaning in music are tied to our perceptions

---

26. Calvin R. Stapert, *My Only Comfort: Death, Deliverance, and Discipleship in the Music of Bach* (Grand Rapids: Eerdmans, 2000), 12–19.

of sound and motion in themselves rather than in their ability to signify external ideas or emotional states. He compared music to an arabesque in art and to the infinite variety of beautiful forms viewed through a kaleidoscope.[27] "Of music," Hanslick wrote, "it is impossible to form any but a musical conception, and it can be comprehended and enjoyed only in and for itself."[28] Hanslick's position is usually called *formalism*, and as an aesthetic theory formalism has had enormous influence on modern developments in music, including set theory.[29]

An early essay on Beethoven's instrumental music by the critic E. T. A. Hoffmann presents a very different view of music and illustrates some of the pros and cons of a kind of interpretation generally referred to as hermeneutics. Here he describes the Trio, Op. 70, no. 1:

> A simple but fruitful theme, songlike, susceptible to the most varied contrapuntal treatments, curtailments, and so forth, forms the basis of each movement; all remaining subsidiary themes and figures are intimately related to the main idea in such a way that the details all interweave, arranging themselves among the instruments in highest unity. Such is the structure of the whole, yet in this artful structure there alternate in restless flight the most marvelous pictures in which joy and grief, melancholy and ecstasy, come side by side or intermingled to the fore. Strange figures begin a merry dance, now floating off into a point of light, now splitting apart, flashing and sparkling, evading and pursuing one another in various combinations, and at the center of the spirit realm thus

27. Eduard Hanslick, *The Beautiful in Music*, ed. Morris Weitz, trans. Gustav Cohen (New York: Liberal Arts Press, 1957), 48.

28. Ibid., 50.

29. Cook, *Guide to Musical Analysis*, 123.

disclosed the intoxicated soul gives ear to the unfamiliar language and understands the most mysterious premonitions that have stirred it.[30]

Hoffmann wrote at a time (1813) when the only way to hear a work such as this was in live performance, and it is easy to see how such flowery and descriptive language could effectively recreate in the mind's ear something of the experience of the piece. Nevertheless, it is difficult to understand what "strange figures begin a merry dance" refers to except as some kind of metaphor for music that we might agree is dance-like. And perhaps nobody but Hoffmann himself could ever quite comprehend or accept his "most mysterious premonitions" that stir the "intoxicated soul." Is it merely Hoffmann's subjective flights of imagination that we read about, or is it Beethoven's trio?

Given that Hoffmann and Beethoven at least knew of one another, it is possible to grant his subjective interpretation a certain historical authority. And Hoffmann's analysis appears to be based on a competent understanding of the musical style, as his references to how themes are introduced and how they interact show. Certainly Hoffmann's contemporaneity and stylistic competence count for something, and his comments do invite us into a particular way of hearing the piece that many musicians will value. But Hoffmann's approach would not likely satisfy a formalist such as Hanslick. As Nicholas Cook observes in a different (though I would say related) context, "Both views are defensible. Which you hold really depends on what sort of person you are."[31]

30. E. T. A. Hoffmann, "Beethoven's Instrumental Music" (1813), trans. Oliver Strunk, in Strunk, *Source Readings in Music History*, 1196–97.
31. Cook, *Guide to Musical Analysis*, 123.

Since the 1980s, musicologists, wanting to establish musical hermeneutics on a more secure theoretical footing, have rethought many of the issues of musical meaning.[32] Cultural and historical context now play a more important role in critical interpretation than in the past, and the formalist's insistence that all that matters is the music itself is being reconsidered. Some old questions are being asked in new ways: Are musical works autonomous? Does music speak for itself? If so, is its meaning transcendent or ineffable? What grounds a listener's subjective responses to music? Can we clarify, within a critical theory of meaning, precisely *how* music is meaningful?

A simple thought experiment may help us to understand how we might answer these questions. Say that a listener finds a passage of instrumental music expressive—that it seems to mean something to her that she identifies as a specific feeling or idea of some kind. Before launching into a description of what that might be, she compares her intuitions about what the piece means with her knowledge of the historical context in which the music was composed—the sorts of things that Hoffmann, as a contemporary of Beethoven, would have taken for granted about music listening, for instance. And, through analysis of the score, she tries to point out those things that happen in the music to which she is attaching significance. A hermeneutic reading of a piece of music thus becomes a reciprocal movement among the listener's subjectivity, the musical facts (including analysis of the score), and the findings of detailed contextual research. Each element in this hermeneutical circle depends on the others, and the resulting interpretations are always provisional and open

32. Lawrence Kramer, *Interpreting Music* (Berkeley: University of California Press, 2011), 1–19.

to further insights, offered in the spirit of humanistic discourse rather than scientific objectivity.[33]

In an award-winning article on an aria from Bach's *St. Matthew Passion*, Naomi Cumming shows how semiotics (theories of linguistic meaning) can underwrite a hermeneutical analysis of a piece of music. She argues that music takes on agency as a subject in its own right, functioning as what semioticians call the "interpretant."[34] This musical subject or persona is the means by which musical signs are joined to what they signify, and the listener engages with this theorized persona in an intersubjective dialogue, identifying with it and experiencing the moods, the narrative, and the affective nuances of the embodied subject heard in the music as it is performed.[35] Explaining the effect of a particularly moving phrase from the violin solo that introduces the aria, Cumming writes, "What is 'known' [by the listener] at the end of the phrase is not a predefined state that can be summarised with the proposition 'the passage expresses sorrow or grief' but an emergent persona, in its provisionality and affective complexity."[36] What the music expresses becomes part of the listener's experience through the mechanism of identification.

The fact that she is discussing an aria from Bach's *St. Matthew Passion* on the text "Erbarme dich, mein Gott, um meiner Zähren willen" (Have mercy, my God, for the sake of my tears) is not lost on Cumming, nor should we miss

---

33. I have not attempted to provide a full critical framework for musical hermeneutics here, but merely to point to some of its key elements. Kramer sums up musical meaning as consisting of "a specific, mutual interplay between musical experience and its contexts" (Lawrence Kramer, *Musical Meaning: Toward a Critical History* [Berkeley: University of California Press, 2002], 8).

34. Naomi Cumming, "The Subjectivities of 'Erbarme Dich,'" *Music Analysis* 16, no. 1 (March 1997): 8, http://www.jstor.org/stable/854112.

35. Ibid., 31, 37.

36. Ibid., 34.

its significance in the context of her interpretation of the music. The aria occurs at a critical point in the passion story: Peter's denial of Christ (Matt. 26:74–75). The entire scene unfolds with a high degree of emotional intensity, which many listeners will experience as feelings of sorrow, grief, and fear. These are the emotions that we would have heard Peter express for himself, if we were in a position to witness his torment, and that we vicariously experience through the music—especially during the short violin solo.

In her article, Cumming explains that her analysis was motivated by a specific occasion in which she joined a small group in an Anglican church in Melbourne, Australia, to hear a recording of the *St. Matthew Passion* on Good Friday. She wanted to know how this music—especially the violin solo—had the effect that it had, both on the people gathered "to meditate" and on herself as she recalled earlier experiences listening to and performing the piece. "Now understanding the text, and standing within a continuing tradition of Christian practice, I cannot readily hear the work in a state of detachment and 'aesthetic distance', yet my experiences with it lead me to ask some questions about my own processes of identification."[37] Identification is, in this instance, the merging of subjectivities: the implied subject in the music, through which meaning happens, and Cumming's own subjectivity—her awareness not only of the music, and the context in which it was composed, but of her own identity as a Christian. "Whichever mode or degree of identification is realised, it remains unavoidable that the text of the aria identifies the music as forming part of a prayer. . . . For a listener who is sympathetic with Bach's theological framework, and subjectively invested in the moment, the aria can constitute *an act of real or symbolic*

37. Ibid., 5.

repentance."[38] Cumming's honesty about the personal and spiritual significance of such engagement is noteworthy. She helps us to understand how musical meaning in a specifically religious work comes to light, subjectively, in a listener's musical experience—especially a shared experience. Rather than eliminate subjectivity, as a formalist critic would, she validates it. And she shows us how faith informs the interpretation without getting sidetracked into mysticism.

My attempt to summarize the many ways in which musicians try to understand musical meaning cannot do much more than whet the appetite for deeper study of the issues. And, although I'm not convinced that a new musical hermeneutics solves all the problems of musical meaning, I have found that the effort to understand the issues, to read and digest the arguments and illustrations, and to try out the various ideas myself as I listen to performances has deepened my connection to music and has led me to a richer appreciation of the awesome gift that God has given us.

FUNCTION

> I should be sorry if I only entertained them, I wish to make them better.
>   —GEORGE FRIDERIC HANDEL[39]

For a musician, the one universal imperative with respect to music is that it must be performed. Musicians want their music to be heard before they want it to be talked about, studied, or analyzed. Contrary to the claims

38. Ibid., 37 (emphasis added).
39. Said to Lord Hay of Kinnoull after the first performance of *Messiah*, as related by James Beattie, letter to the Reverend Dr. Laing, May 25, 1780. Quoted in Donald Burrows, *Handel: Messiah* (Cambridge: Cambridge University Press, 1991), 28.

of the most extreme kinds of formalism, music needs to be realized in sound; it needs to be heard.

But music is much more than either scores or performances. Recent scholarship has emphasized that music is a *social practice*—that it exists not so much as a thing to be contemplated or as a score to be realized in performance, but as a process.[40] The totality of music cannot be encompassed by "work" or "composition," although these terms remain important through their association with classical music as an art form. The idea of "work" leaves out a great deal of what people experience as music every day: what they make up on the spot, for instance, or the mash-ups and remixes of recent popular music. And the way in which any kind of music is used will determine, in part, what it means to its users. Once again, Bonnie Wade helps to amplify this insight by considering the many ways that people use music: "People make music useful in so many ways that one can think of—socially, as a mode of interaction or to create a romantic mood; politically, to control or unite; spiritually, for sacred expression and worship; economically, to make a living; medically, for soothing or healing; and so many more ways."[41] To this list we can add individual listening and contemplation of classical or jazz music in the privacy of one's home through the mediation of one's mp3 player or some other technology. These forms of listening are also a function of music and do some form of cultural work (relaxation, enjoyment, aesthetic appreciation—even just getting the chores done).

The study of the way that music is used—its musical function—has both historical and cultural aspects. One can therefore speak in general of a *historical musicology*,

40. Wade, *Thinking Musically*, 6.
41. Ibid., 18.

or music history, in which scholars attempt to reconstruct music and musical practices in the lives of people from the past, and one can also speak of a *cultural musicology*, in which the cultural work that music does is studied using ethnography and other research methods derived from the social sciences.[42] In many respects these fields overlap—cultural musicologists are interested in history and vice versa. Whichever orientation characterizes a musicologist's work, however, the questions that are often the most interesting have to do with the use or function of music, what purposes it served or serves, and how people think about what music is and what it means to them.

Historical musicology, my own field of research, is usually associated with classical music and its canonic composers and works. But one of its most noteworthy achievements is the early music-performance movement of the twentieth century, which transformed the musical world's understanding of the integration of performance with scholarship. Scholars working on pre-eighteenth-century music joined forces with performers (and often the scholars *were* performers) to think about how past ways of hearing and performing music might affect performances in the present and to apply this thinking to "early music": everything from medieval troubadour songs to seventeenth-century opera. Even the music of Mozart and Beethoven has been rethought—sometimes with controversial results—as the performance practice of early music has encroached on more traditional repertory. Concepts such as authenticity became hotly contested zones of scholarly activity, with conflicting ideas and performances

---

42. I am using the term "cultural musicology" here in a different sense from Lawrence Kramer, for whom it is synonymous with the "new" musicology of the 1990s (see Lawrence Kramer, "Subjectivity Rampant! Music, Hermeneutics, and History," in *The Cultural Study of Music: A Critical Introduction*, ed. Martin Clayton, Trevor Herbert, and Richard Middleton [New York: Routledge, 2003], 125).

contributing to a chaotic, but vital, musical practice.[43] In some ways, the early music movement epitomizes what a social practice is: a dynamic musical world in which musicians of all kinds exchange music and musical techniques, question assumptions about music and performance, and think about what it all might mean.

Perhaps in modern Western culture music has no greater function than to express identity. Individuals collect their own music, share it with their friends, and use it to communicate their values or to denote their affiliation with a social group.[44] Music also helps to establish corporate identities and is used to advertise products and to manipulate the human desire for membership and status. Unfortunately, music can also divide people from one another, creating boundaries between people of different ages, ethnicities, or socioeconomic statuses. Musicologists are increasingly interested in how music is used for constructing and maintaining identities, how borders between groups are reinforced by certain musical styles, and how border crossings create the conditions for new stylistic developments and fusions.[45]

Recognizing that music is a social practice also offers us new ways to think about some thorny issues affecting church musicians. Many Christians are concerned about the potential effects of poor musical choices in worship, and so often these concerns turn into debates over musical style. But rather than separate musical styles from their social function, it seems more profitable for us to focus on what we're asking music to do and whether a particular kind of music actually fits well with how we're using it.[46] Music,

43. Nicholas Kenyon, ed., *Authenticity and Early Music: A Symposium* (Oxford: Oxford University Press, 1988), 6–7.

44. Wade, *Thinking Musically*, 18–19.

45. Ibid., 161–94.

46. It is not my intention here to argue the aesthetic merits of one style over

Calvin wrote, "has a secret and almost incredible power to move our hearts in one way or another. Wherefore we must be the more diligent in ruling it in such a manner that it may be useful to us and in no way pernicious."[47] Calvin recognized that decisions about music need to be made in wise and thoughtful ways, respecting both its power *and* its usefulness in worship. I have found that well-trained musicians can help congregations to understand the difference between music that is well crafted and suited to its task and music that will be a distraction or worse. As congregations begin to think about music as a social practice, perhaps real consensus about music can be achieved, and it can be restored to the purposes that God intended. Clearly this calls for biblically informed spiritual discernment and much prayer.

CONCLUSION: A DISCIPLINE THROUGH WHICH TO FLOURISH

It should be evident at this point that the discipline of music involves many rich conversations and an abundance of perspectives. As we peer into the world of performers, composers, and musicologists, listen to what they care about, and consider what that might mean for us as Christian musicians, we encounter a living discipline made up of musicians who are serious about their work. In my view, what makes the learning that we are seeking to do *faithful* is our attitude toward the discipline and our willingness, by faith, to be responsible for it. This means asking the questions that need to be asked, participating in the

another, but I do find the concept of "fittingness" helpful as we think about music in worship. See Nicholas Wolterstorff, *Art in Action: Toward a Christian Aesthetic* (Grand Rapids: Eerdmans, 1980), 167.

47. Calvin, *Geneva Psalter*, 366.

conversations that musicians are having with each other, and listening to the insights of other disciplines so that we can think musically in ways that meet the needs of our time. The attitude that I have in mind couples diligence with grace and effort with gratitude. It locates the outcomes of faithful learning not only in the *view* that we have of things, but also in the doing of them, as we are mindful always of our tendency as fallen human beings to take pride in our knowledge and ability rather than to approach the tasks at hand with humility.

In a music literature course in college I read Aaron Copland's little book, *What to Listen for in Music*.[48] You will recall that I, like many music majors, was impatient with required courses in music theory and music history, which, to my way of thinking at the time, impeded my progress as a musician. Rather than reinforce these tendencies, Copland's book inscribed *music* onto my mind—music not as mere technique or style, but as a way of life. In short, music became a calling. This book enabled me to see beyond my assumptions about how to get ahead in music, and it opened my eyes to the fact that, like any great liberal arts discipline, the study of music offered an abundance of new associations and ideas as well as the prospect of rich, fertile soil in which to be planted. My hope is that, by considering how order, meaning, and function shape conversations about music, students will realize, as I did, that the discipline of music is wider in scope than they might have thought. To engage the discipline fully is to commit to something larger than ourselves—larger than any single person could ever comprehend.

Faithful learning takes us beyond adding a few prayers before a performance or writing *Soli Deo Gloria* on a score; it is an all-in, fully engaged commitment to serve God by

---

48. Aaron Copland, *What to Listen for in Music* (New York: McGraw-Hill, 1957).

becoming a steward of one of his greatest gifts to human beings, a commitment that we offer by faith. And what we find is that the discipline of music pays back above and beyond all our expectations. As we enter into this study openly and expectantly—ready to receive what God freely gives out of the richness of his being as Father, Son, and Holy Spirit—we experience something of God's abundance, his plenitude. It then remains for us to develop the discipline in fruitful ways and to share the expertise, the insights, and the judgments that we form through that work with our neighbors. Our work in the discipline of music cannot be merely an end in itself; as faithful stewards of the science and art of music, we want to leave our studios and our offices and to go out into the world that God loves, to listen and to act as his musical agents of renewal.

DISCUSSION QUESTIONS

1. In what sense(s) can music be considered a "gift" of God? What responsibilities do people have with respect to this gift?
2. Why did Calvin warn against an overly optimistic view of music? What kinds of generalizations about the effects of the fall on music can be misleading? Where do those effects show up most clearly?
3. What is the benefit of beginning a discussion of music by thinking about who musicians are and what they do?
4. What, according to the author, characterizes engagement with the "discipline" of music?
5. Which three practices make up the academic discipline of music? Are there other practices associated with music that you can think of?
6. Can the discipline of music be comprehended by means of one of the three practices alone? Why or why not?

7. What is the value of using "order, meaning, and function" to provide a framework for conversations about music? In addition to those already quoted by the author, can you think of passages in Scripture that offer insight into these concepts or refine our sense of how they apply to music making?

8. Which ancient ideas about music have had the greatest impact on Western musical theory?

9. What distinguishes a rational account of music from an empirical one?

10. What characteristics of music make conversations about musical meaning difficult? How have musicians responded to these difficulties? Why does that matter?

11. How might a musician's faith inform his or her interpretation of a piece of sacred music? Could the same apply to non-sacred music?

12. In what ways can thinking about music as a social practice help us to better understand music itself?

13. What distinguishes "historical" from "cultural" musicology? What unites these two scholarly orientations?

14. What characterizes faithful learning in the discipline of music?

15. What difference might it make to you, as you think about your own study of music, to envision yourself as a musical agent of renewal in God's world?

SERIES AFTERWORD

Christians are called to enter, engage, and cultivate every sphere of lawful human activity. And increasingly, in our modern age, this calling requires us to receive training in specialized disciplines beyond the high school level. We must enter colleges, universities, and technical schools to develop knowledge and skills that will equip us to engage in good, even necessary cultural activities in the humanities, the sciences, technology, and the fine arts. But many Christian families are justifiably anxious about sending their children into the modern secular academy to obtain such training; many assume that the norms and beliefs under which the modern academic disciplines operate are at odds with the values their children have been taught in their homes and churches.

While it is important for Christians to instill in one another a biblical framework—a "Christian worldview"— that will help us to understand and interpret what we learn in faithful ways, it is also necessary to consider the fact that the modern academic disciplines are good gifts from a good and gracious God. And they are each packed with insights—"common grace insights"—that can and should be used for the good of the world and the glory of God.

Faithful Learning is a series of modest-sized booklets that provide Christian invitations to the modern academic disciplines. Each volume will introduce students—along with teachers and other educational professionals—to a distinct academic discipline and will challenge readers to grapple with the foundational ideas, practices, and applications found in each of them. The authors of these booklets are highly trained Christian scholars who operate under the assumption that, when understood rightly, each of their disciplines holds the potential for students to cultivate a deeper love for God and for their neighbors. It is our hope and prayer that these booklets will be used by Christians to engage their academic studies with greater confidence and understanding, and that they will thereby be more equipped to *learn faithfully* about whatever pursuit or sphere of human activity God is calling them to.

Jay D. Green

BIBLIOGRAPHY

Begbie, Jeremy S. *Resounding Truth: Christian Wisdom in the World of Music.* Grand Rapids: Baker Academic, 2007.

Burkholder, J. Peter, Donald Jay Grout, and Claude V. Palisca. *A History of Western Music.* 8th ed. New York: W. W. Norton, 2010.

Burrows, Donald. *Handel: Messiah.* Cambridge: Cambridge University Press, 1991.

Calvin, John. "Epistle to the Reader." *The Geneva Psalter. 1543.* Translated by Oliver Strunk. In Strunk, *Source Readings in Music History,* 364–67.

Cook, Nicholas. *A Guide to Musical Analysis.* London: J. M. Dent & Sons, 1987. Reprint, New York: W. W. Norton, 1992.

Copland, Aaron. *What to Listen for in Music.* New York: McGraw-Hill, 1957.

Cumming, Naomi. "The Subjectivities of 'Erbarme Dich.'" *Music Analysis* 16, no. 1 (March 1997): 5–44. http://www.jstor.org /stable/854112.

David, Hans T., and Arthur Mendel, eds. *The Bach Reader: A Life of Johann Sebastian Bach in Letters and Documents.* Revised edition. New York: W. W. Norton, 1966.

DeMol, Karen A. *Sound Stewardship: How Shall Christians Think About Music?* Sioux Center, IA: Dordt College Press, 1999.

Dillard, Annie. *Teaching a Stone to Talk: Expeditions and Encounters.* New York: Harper Perennial, 1992.

Forte, Allen, and Steven E. Gilbert. *Introduction to Schenkerian Analysis.* New York: W. W. Norton, 1982.

Hanslick, Eduard. *The Beautiful in Music.* Edited by Morris Weitz. Translated by Gustav Cohen. New York: Liberal Arts Press, 1957.

Hoffmann, E. T. A. "Beethoven's Instrumental Music." 1813. Translated by Oliver Strunk. In Strunk, *Source Readings in Music History,* 1193–98.

Johnson, Bruce, and Martin Cloonan. *Dark Side of the Tune: Popular Music and Violence.* Farnham, UK: Ashgate, 2009.

Karp, Theodore C. "Music." In *The Seven Liberal Arts in the Middle Ages,* edited by David L. Wagner, 169–95. Bloomington, IN: Indiana University Press, 1986.

Kenyon, Nicholas. *Authenticity and Early Music: A Symposium.* Oxford: Oxford University Press, 1988.

Kilmer, Anne D., Richard L. Crocker, and Robert R. Brown. *Sounds from Silence: Recent Discoveries in Ancient Near Eastern Music.* Recorded lecture demonstration. BTNK 101, 1976. 33 1/3 rpm LP and 2 compact discs.

Kostka, Stefan, and Dorothy Payne. *Tonal Harmony: With an Introduction to Twentieth-Century Music.* 6th ed. Boston: McGraw-Hill Higher Education, 2009.

Kramer, Lawrence. *Interpreting Music.* Berkeley: University of California Press, 2011.

———. *Musical Meaning: Toward a Critical History.* Berkeley: University of California Press, 2002.

———. "Subjectivity Rampant! Music, Hermeneutics, and History." In *The Cultural Study of Music: A Critical Introduction,* edited by Martin Clayton, Trevor Herbert, and Richard Middleton, 124–35. New York: Routledge, 2003.

Luther, Martin. *D. Martin Luthers Werke: Tischreden.* 6 vols. Weimar: Hermann Böhlau Nachfolger, 1912–21. http://www.archive.org/details/werketischreden10204luthuoft.

Machaut, Guillaume de. *Oeuvres de Guillaume de Machaut.* 3 vols. Edited by Ernest Hoepffner. Paris: Librairie de Firmin-Didot, 1908. http://www.archive.org/details/uvresdeguillaum00guilgoog.

Rosen, Charles. *The Classical Style: Haydn, Mozart, Beethoven.* Expanded edition. New York: W. W. Norton, 1998.

Stapert, Calvin R. *My Only Comfort: Death, Deliverance, and Discipleship in the Music of Bach.* Grand Rapids: Eerdmans, 2000.

Straus, Joseph N. *Introduction to Post-Tonal Theory.* 2nd ed. Upper Saddle River, NJ: Prentice Hall, 2000.

Strunk, Oliver, ed. *Source Readings in Music History.* Revised edition. Leo Treitler, general editor. New York: W. W. Norton, 1998.

Wade, Bonnie C. *Thinking Musically: Experiencing Music, Expressing Culture.* 3rd ed. New York: Oxford University Press, 2012.

Weber, Gottfried. *Theory of Musical Composition: Treated with a View to a Naturally Consecutive Arrangement of Topics.* Translated by James F. Warner. 2 vols. Boston: Oliver Ditson, 1846.

Wolters-Fredlund, Benita. "Experiencing Beauty in the Music of the Holocaust." *The Cresset* 72, no. 4 (Easter 2009): 21–31. http://thecresset.org/2009/Easter/wolters-fredlund.html.

Wolterstorff, Nicholas. *Art in Action: Toward a Christian Aesthetic.* Grand Rapids: Eerdmans, 1980.